Deliverance From Sexual Dreams

Johannes Tefo

Published by Johannes Tefo, 2024.

Also by Johannes Tefo

Family spiritual Warfare Books

Generational Curses And Spiritual Warfare: Spiritual Strategies & Principles Of Victory Against Evil Strongholds

Youth's Guide To Spiritual Warfare

A Women's Guide To Spiritual Warfare

Standalone

Deliver Your Soul From Evil

Overcoming Spirit Of Stagnation

The 24: Prophetic Word For This Season 2024 And Beyond

Michael For Warfare

Territorial Spirits: Overcome Evil Strongholds in Your Life And Take Over Your Community With Strategic Warfare And Winning Prayers

Prayers Against Suicide Spirit

Spiritual Warfare When Enough is Enough

Identity In Christ

Prayers Against Satanic Networks

The Workplace You Need: Spiritual Warfare Prayers That Silence Evil Powers At Your Workplace.

Deliverance From Mind Control: Be Free And Delivered From Every Marine Demons Of Mind Control

Times Getting Hard: Scriptures Of Comfort For Hard Days

Battle In The Sea: How To Tackle Spiritual Warfare And Win The Battle

Freedom: Deliverance Of Souls From Captivity

A Dedicated Prayer Lifestyle: Simple Tips To Effective Prayer Lifestyle

Deliverance From Sexual Dreams

Sexual Lust, Demons, And Impurity

Redefined By Fire: Unleashing The Power Of The Holy Spirit Within.

Table of Contents

Deliverance from sex in dreams.

I grew up in a Pentecostal church where healing and deliverance were administered through water cleansing. I remember one night, I had a dream of seeing a young woman entering my room, and someone was shouting saying "Do not let her enter your room". From that time, I have started having encounters with women sleeping with me in my dreams, and waking up feeling dirty and shameful because I woke up with an orgasm all over me.

These are strange things that happen at night. The Psalmist in Psalm 91 says "Thou shalt not be afraid for the terror by night; nor for the arrow that flieth by day", meaning, there are arrows that fly during the night and day, and these arrows are from the evil one. Arrows may be sicknesses, diseases, poverty, unemployment, etc. these are the fiery darts that the enemy throws us at to weaken the spirit of man and women.

I have to say that, I have had my share with sexual demons of the night defiling my soul and body. I later realized that, when there is a door open in your life, there is an invitation to all kinds of spirits.

Your body in spirit is a house. Your body is the church or the temple. If the temple has no lamp in it, which is the light of God, darkness is bound to cover you. Apostle Paul says *"I beseech you therefore, brethren, by the mercies of God, that ye present your bodies a living sacrifice, holy, acceptable unto God, which is your reasonable service".*

Now the body is the tabernacle of God. Now the body is the temple of the Holy Spirit. Thus Christ had to say "The kingdom of God is within you".

It is a depressing journey when you are in a battle with the unseen spirit that even goes as far as defiling your spirit man sexually. You even feel the impact physically, some are raped, some are strangled in sleep, and some even spirits appear physically.

There is hope in the Lord for those who are dark season. This is a serious issue that even the church does not entertain since many do not believe that there are spirits that have intercourse with people. If in the time of Noah, Angels slept with women, then it means even today spirits can do the same. There is nothing new under the sun.

We are reaching the point where the sexual revolution is celebrated no matter the age. This is the age where black and white are seen as the same thing. The age where the rampage of evil is all-time high. Deception is taking its toll in all sectors of life. Church is now a refuge for wickedness. These are the times foreseen by the prophets of old—the love of many shall grow weary, people shall become the lovers of themselves and sexual sins shall rampage the whole world.

I wrote this book with a sincere heart to help you overcome the power of evil of the night. Over the years, the sexual demons of the night have been named Incubus and Succubus;

Females – incubus (Latin – to lie upon)
Males – succubus (Latin – to lie under)

These spirits are spirits that seek to have sexual intercourse with men and women during the night hours. Incubus is described as a spirit being that comes to have intimate relationships with women while they are asleep while

Succubus is described as a spirit being that comes to have relationships with men in their sleep. These dream visitors are called spirit husbands and spirit wives.

Deliverance happens when you receive the revelation of the Holy Spirit about how these demons got through you. While watching pornography, fornicating or masturbating may be the ultimate gateway to a spiritual husband and spiritual wife, there are other factors such as idol worship, covenanted to demons, or witchcraft practices that can seduce these spirits to be part of your life.

At the end of this book, you will be inspired to seek deliverance or rather, self-deliver yourself in the name of the Lord. self-delivered is as powerful as ministers of the gospel, the most important thing you will ever need is faith. Faith pleases God. And He acts when the move of your life is faith.

We can exhort, encourage, edify or even offer prayers as much, but as the end of the day, the just shall live by faith. Practice your God-given faith by the grace of God. He is the reward of those who diligently seek Him.

The Word of God.

A living soul without the Word of God is powerless. A man does not live by bread alone, but by every word that precedes out of the mouth of God. Everything that comes out of the mouth of God brings life. He spoke, there was life on earth, and the heavens and earth became lively by His command. By His command, He establishes.

The power is in His word to establish all things under the sun. in a certain scripture it is written "He holds all things together by the power of the Word of His mouth". Jesus Christ defeated the Devil after a 40-day fast through the Word of God. Surprisingly, fasting and prayer did not defeat him. The devil appeared after 40 days and tempted him, it is only when you say it is written the devil flees for a season.

There is no smooth riding and sailing in this world, the devil only leaves you for a season, where he is just know that he is plotting the next move about your life. It is through the grace of the Living God that we can defeat him. Without the Holy Spirit in us, we are no match to the fallen beings.

After these beings fell, they made it their mission to attack not only humans but the angels of God too. There is a kingdom up in the sky, in the second heaven, set up to capture the souls of men and restrict the transaction of angels and humanity on earth. As the body of Christ, we all ought to wage spiritual warfare prayers and live a life pleasing to God that the enemy will have no accusation before the throne of God.

In the spirit realm, there is an ongoing fight, it is a legal fight between the body of Christ and the enemy, Satan. As we are purchased by the blood of Jesus Christ, let us hold onto to the calling till the end of the time. Through the precious blood of Christ, men have power over the works of the enemy and can live an overcoming life.

The overcoming of life happens when the Word is in you. When the kingdom of God is in you.

Hebrews 4:12 For the word of God is quick, and powerful, and sharper than any
two-edged sword, piercing even to the dividing asunder of soul and spirit, and of
the joints and marrow, and is a discerner of the thoughts and intents of the heart.

The Word is powerful enough to defend you against the wiles of the enemy. The tempter has no way to overcome you when the Living Word of God breath and lives in you. The spirit and soul is quickened by the Word of God.

When the spirit man rules over your soul and your body, you have defeated your flesh. Flesh keeps us in bondage while the spirit of freedom in Christ brings us into liberty. Holy Spirit is the spirit of liberty. Any area of your life that is in bondage is not submitted under the will of the Holy Spirit.

10 And if Christ be in you, the body is dead because of sin; but the Spirit is
life because of righteousness.
11 But if the Spirit of him that raised up Jesus from the dead dwell in you,
he that raised up Christ from the dead shall also quicken your mortal bodies by

Christ preached the Word when He was on earth. He taught more than He healed or delivered people from demons. He taught about the kingdom of God, the kingdom of heaven, this was his overall message. The message of repentance which leads to the entrance into the kingdom of God. Likewise, John taught the same message.

He taught as He knew the power of the Word. People can get delivered from time to time but it is also a high price to maintain that deliverance. Thus, the Word is the pillar of all, the Word stands, and the word produces fruits and great results. Everything that has to be maintain in line with the kingdom of God, it is kept through the power of the Word.

The kingdom is the kingdom of words. We wage wars through words, we worship with words, we pray with words, we study the words, etc. the kingdom in you is the Word and the spirit of God—the Holy Spirit of truth.

When we are dealing with evil spirits, evil altars, and marine powers of sex demons, the Word, and the zealous prayer life is the principle of engaging the enemy and winning the warfare. Because it is a war, demons hate you but fear you only when you walk in power and authority.

Destructive fire prayers will do very good jo when contending with the marine powers as most of spiritual husband and spiritual wife resides in the water. These are the demons under the rulership of the queen of the coast, the women who sit upon the water. The is so much evil that is happening in the underwater realm.

These spirits draw power from men and women—feed themselves with the blood of men and women. Do not be fooled, the kingdom of darkness thrives itself with the power of sex. They know that sex is holy and sacred, therefore, the enemy uses it to bring the fall of humanity.

When you have sex outside the will of God, you are trading with your destiny as a men or woman. And you have opened the dark portal which the demons from the spirit world will use it to build their stronghold. It is all about territory in the realm of spirits.

If the spirit of God is not in you, the spirit of Satan will be. I was shocked one day when I was in spirit seeing the demons collecting used condoms after sexual intercourse, while some collecting every bit of semen of men and women, it was clear to me that sexual intercourse is done outside the will of the Holy Father, there are repercussions.

1 Corinthians 6:18 - *"Flee fornication. Every sin that a man doeth is without the body; but he that committeth fornication sinneth against his own body."*

. . . .

Galatians 5:19 - "*Now the works of the flesh are manifest, which are these; Adultery, fornication, uncleanness, lasciviousness.*"

1 Thessalonians 4:3 - "*For this is the will of God, even your sanctification, that ye should abstain from fornication.*"

FORNICATION, MASTURBATION, homosexuality, and adultery will always be the hot spot for marine spirits and marine agents to infiltrate the lives of many believers and non-believers alike.

I have many Christians in my village who went without luck in banishing these sexual demons out of their life. And their lives are the living proof that the powers of darkness can limit your great things in life. A life of no progress, non-achievement life, poverty, financial struggle, and money just randomly vanishes in thin air, is the real proof of the works of evil spirits behind.

A student of the Bible.

It is vital to elevate your prayer lifestyle when trouble mounts up. If you used to pray for 5 minutes, double it up. The student of the bible is a person of prayer inspired and moved by the Word of God. David inspired himself in the Lord and continued with the journey of faith even at point it seemed impossible.

Psalm 119:24 Thy testimonies also are my delight and my counsellors.

The law of the Lord became his counselor. God is the rewarder of those who are faithful in His Word, He rewards them for their faith, dedication, and their zealousness. Jesus Christ was zealous for the house of God—the man of righteousness. Righteous men hate even the stain of sin. They live a life pleasing to God.

Psalm 69:9 For the zeal of thine house hath eaten me up; and the reproaches of them
that reproached thee are fallen upon me.

The students of the bible have a zeal for the kingdom of God upon the earth. they have a zeal for the mind and the will of God. They are God pleasers rather than men-pleasers.

8 It is better to trust in the LORD than to put confidence in man.

9 It is better to trust in the LORD than to put confidence in princes.

Psalm 118:8-9.

The Lord God the Holy Father in the name of Jesus Christ is who we look for, those in authority may help us here and there, but they have their limit, God is limitless. If you want to go far in life, trust the Lord God at all times.

In Africa and most parts of the world, we have made religious men to be demi-gods or junior gods to the point where we no longer look up to Jesus Christ, who is the author and the finisher of our faith. Apostles, prophets, bishops, and pastors are drawing congregants to themselves instead of pointing them to their maker, He who made the heavens and the earth.

Keep your faith pure, walk in the truth of the common faith, and work out your own salvation in the name of the Lord. With all kinds of prayers, we should seek the face of the Lord and pray according to the will and the mind of the Holy Spirit.

Praying in the Holy Ghost will strengthen our faith. The weak man is strengthened when we stir ourselves up in the Holy faith mentioned by Jude.

3 Beloved, when I gave all diligence to write unto you of the common
salvation, it was needful for me to write unto you, and exhort you that ye should
earnestly contend for the faith which was once delivered unto the saints.
Jude 1:3.
20 But ye, beloved, building up yourselves on your most holy faith, praying
in the Holy Ghost,
21 Keep yourselves in the love of God, looking for the mercy of our Lord
Jesus Christ unto eternal life.
Jude 1:20-21.

These two scriptures exhorts us to earnestly contend for the faith which was once delivered unto the saints. The common salvation of the undiluted kingdom of God. The gospel does not please men but convicts them to follow Christ in righteousness and holiness. In all readiness of peace and meekness.

At the end of the race, it is the holy faith that will keep us. Faith is a forever trend; it does not come out of fashion. God will honor faith. He then rewards faith. And faith is the result of the Word of God.

It is written;

8 But what saith it? The word is nigh thee, even in thy mouth, and in thy
heart: that is, the word of faith, which we preach;
9 That if thou shalt confess with thy mouth the Lord Jesus, and shalt believe
in thine heart that God hath raised him from the dead, thou shalt be saved.
10 For with the heart man believeth unto righteousness; and with the mouth
confession is made unto salvation.
11 For the scripture saith, Whosoever believeth on him shall not be ashamed.
Romans 10:8-11.
Romans 10:17 So then faith cometh by hearing, and hearing by the word of God.

Total deliverance comes when we immerse ourselves in the Word and maintenance of our deliverance also comes when the Word is in us. It is critical and highly important to be a student of the bible. Faith is quickened by the Word.

Hear the Word, and live.

*John 6:63 It is the spirit that quickeneth; the flesh profiteth nothing: the words that I
speak unto you, they are spirit, and they are life.*

Study prayer patterns of the bible.

S incere prayers that come from the heart of a believer have no formula. The Holy Spirit in us leads us to prayer the prayer that aligns with the will of God. Any prayer that is outside the will of God will surely be disappointed. However, there are a few prayers that we can learn and model in the bible.

Jesus Christ taught His disciples how to pray. John the Baptist also taught his disciples to pray. In the old covenant, God taught Moses the Aaronic priesthood blessing prayer (Number 6:24).

Right prayers will always be answered by the righteous Father. The author and the finisher of our faith is Jesus Christ. By all means, we ought to follow the example Jesus Christ set. Paul says *"Follow me as I follow Christ"*.

Back in the day, I copied all the prayers men and women of God prayed in the bible, and diligently studied them, and how they were answered. And I concluded that heartfelt prayers will never be despised. Above that, prayer that has its stand on the Word was always answered.

Here I have four different prayers that we will pray. These prayers have been in my heart for so long, and hopefully, at some point, I will analyze them in articles and books.

Aron Priesthood blessing prayer

23 Speak unto Aaron and unto his sons, saying, On this wise ye shall bless
the children of Israel, saying unto them,
24 The LORD bless thee, and keep thee:

25 The LORD make his face shine upon thee, and be gracious unto thee:

26 The LORD lift up his countenance upon thee, and give thee peace.

27 And they shall put my name upon the children of Israel, and I will bless them.

. . . .

The Lord's prayer.

Our Father which art in heaven,
Hallowed be thy name.
10 Thy kingdom come, Thy will be done in earth, as it is in heaven.
11 Give us this day our daily bread.
12 And forgive us our debts, as we forgive our debtors.
13 And lead us not into temptation, but deliver us from evil: For thine is the
kingdom, and the power, and the glory, for ever. Amen.

Psalm 90

1 Lord, thou hast been our dwelling place in all generations.
2 Before the mountains were brought forth, or ever thou hadst formed the
earth and the world, even from everlasting to everlasting, thou art God.
3 Thou turnest man to destruction; and sayest, Return, ye children of men.
4 For a thousand years in thy sight are but as yesterday when it is past, and
as a watch in the night.

5 Thou carriest them away as with a flood; they are as a sleep: in the
morning they are like grass which groweth up.
6 In the morning it flourisheth, and groweth up; in the evening it is cut
down, and withereth.
7 For we are consumed by thine anger, and by thy wrath are we
troubled.
8 Thou hast set our iniquities before thee, our secret sins in the light of thy
countenance.
9 For all our days are passed away in thy wrath: we spend our years as a tale
that is told.
10 The days of our years are threescore years and ten; and if by rea-son of
strength they be fourscore years, yet is their strength labour and
sorrow; for it is
soon cut off, and we fly away.
11 Who knoweth the power of thine anger? even according to thy fear, so is
thy wrath.
12 So teach us to number our days, that we may apply our hearts unto
wisdom.
13 Return, O LORD, how long? and let it repent thee concerning thy
servants.
14 O satisfy us early with thy mercy; that we may rejoice and be glad all our

days.
15 Make us glad according to the days wherein thou hast afflicted us, and
the years wherein we have seen evil.
16 Let thy work appear unto thy servants, and thy glory unto their children.
17 And let the beauty of the LORD our God be upon us: and establish thou
the work of our hands upon us; yea, the work of our hands establish thou it.

Psalm 91

1 He that dwelleth in the secret place of the most High shall abide under the

shadow of the Almighty.

2 I will say of the LORD, He is my refuge and my fortress: my God; in him

will I trust.

3 Surely he shall deliver thee from the snare of the fowler, and from the

noisome pestilence.

4 He shall cover thee with his feathers, and under his wings shalt thou trust:

his truth shall be thy shield and buckler.

5 Thou shalt not be afraid for the terror by night; nor for the arrow that

flieth by day;

6 Nor for the pestilence that walketh in darkness; nor for the de-struction that

wasteth at noonday.

7 A thousand shall fall at thy side, and ten thousand at thy right hand; but it

shall not come nigh thee.

8 Only with thine eyes shalt thou behold and see the reward of the wicked.

9 Because thou hast made the LORD, which is my refuge, even the most

High, thy habitation;

10 There shall no evil befall thee, neither shall any plague come nigh thy

dwelling.

11 For he shall give his angels charge over thee, to keep thee in all
thy ways.
12 They shall bear thee up in their hands, lest thou dash thy foot
against a
stone.
13 Thou shalt tread upon the lion and adder: the young lion and
the dragon
shalt thou trample under feet.
14 Because he hath set his love upon me, therefore will I deliver
him: I will
set him on high, because he hath known my name.
15 He shall call upon me, and I will answer him: I will be with
him in
trouble; I will deliver him, and honour him.
16 With long life will I satisfy him, and show him my salvation.

ARON BLESSING PRAYER

This is a blessing prayer mainly used by Jewish rabbis to bless the children. You can speak this blessing over your life, every time you walk up before you go to work, school, or study, or even before you travel, speak this prayer over your life. God performs his word.

You are washed by the blood of Jesus Christ, therefore, you are a priest and a king. This is the priestly prayer of blessing for Aron. The nation of Israel prospered in the hand of Aron through this prayer. This prayer comes from God. God taught Moses, and Moses gave it to Aron.

The Lord's Prayer.

This is the perfect prayer that Jesus taught his disciples. It teaches us to honor the name of the Lord, bless the name of the Lord, and hallow it before we petition our own needs. Thus David says *"Enter into his gates with thanksgiving, and into his courts with praise: be thankful unto him, and bless his name"*.

Christ teaches us that the main purpose of prayer is to call the will of God to happen on earth and in our lives. The selfish prayer is when you want your will to overrule the will of God. It is important to study the Word of God, to know his mind and His will upon our lives, so that we can foster that idea.

We have prayed this prayer all our lives but many do not grasp the power behind this prayer. This is not a religious or traditional prayer but the power of God. This prayer is even prophetic in nature, it is the prayer that prophecy the will of God on earth, not the will of men. This is the heart of Christ, that we should be not about our own business but about the Father's business.

Psalm 69:9 For the zeal of thine house hath eaten me up; and the reproaches of them
that reproached thee are fallen upon me.

Psalms 90 & 91

These are deliverance prayers. Meditate on these Psalms, pray them, sing them, proclaim them, and memorize them.

In the spirit realm, you are destroying the strongholds of evil through this deliverance Psalms.

Psalms are full of deliverance prayers, you can also add Psalm 35, Psalm 144, Psalm 140, and Psalm 24 on your list of deliverance songs.

Prayer mixed with fasting usually yields results fast. There are different kinds of fasting you can undertake, though, allowing the Holy Spirit to lead you. But you can start small with 1 day, 3 days, or even 7 days. 21 days and 40 days fasting are serious prayers that, if you do not have the legs for 3 to 7 days, you will be disappointed with an incomplete mission.

Mathews 17:21 Howbeit this kind goeth not out but by prayer and fasting.

Prayer of deliverance.

Heavenly Father, I come to You in honest brokenness and repentance about my involvement in opening doors to the sex kingdoms of this world and Satan and for allowing the Power called Asmodee to control my will and therefore my sexual desires. I ask Your forgiveness, Father, and I ask You to cleanse me of all defilement with Your Holy Fire.

I confess of letting down my guard over my thought life, of the sin of prayerlessness, of the sin of slackness and laziness in my spiritual walk with You. I ask Your forgiveness for not wearing the Helmet of Salvation over my thought life, for opening up to judging and criticizing the Church and other believers. I confess for not wearing the Full Armor of God according to Ephesians 6. Please forgive me, Lord.

I ask Your forgiveness, Holy Spirit, because I did not heed Your warnings. I hardened my heart to Your prompting as You tried to get my attention to stop what I was doing. Forgive me for having my conscience seared, from turning away from the Truth, giving attention to deluding and seducing spirits and doctrines that demons teach (1 Tim 4:2). Please help me to regain the sensitivity of my conscience and spirit to heed Your voice again.

Father, I ask that You will grant me the HOPE as I repent and come to know the Truth about how You really feel about this sin. Of how I have grieved You and those that I love, so that I can come to my senses and escape out of the snare of the devil, having been held captive by him (2 Tim 2:25, 26).

I call upon Your Name Yahweh Jehoram – Raised up by God and I pray in the Name of Jesus that You will restore me and raise me up and establish me in Your Kingdom. Lord, I now choose to welcome the Truth into my life. I choose to love the Truth so that I may be saved, cleansed and sanctified from the lawless one/ the spirit of the anti-christ. Set me free from this great power and delusive marvels, from his unlimited seduction to evil and all his wicked deception.

Father, please remove this misleading influence, a working of error and a strong delusion that made me believe what is false because I did not adhere to, trust in, and rely on the Truth, but instead took pleasure in unrighteousness (2 Thess 2: 9-12). I confess opening doors to all the different websites, the one leading me on to the next and the voices calling me in the spirit.

Father, I confess for creating and building an altar in the spirit where Satan was worshipped (the chair, table, room, space – all must be cleansed, altar destroyed). I ask you to cleanse and purify all physical aspects used in this worship and ask you to destroy this ungodly altar in Jesus Name.

I petition You to cleanse the contact point of the hand with mouse, fingertips, handeye- co-ordination, defilement of eye-gate. Father, we fire all gatekeepers assigned over these eye-gates and ask you to cleanse these gateways from all defilement (also my hands).

Father, I petition that you gather all parts of my spirit and soul held captive in the kingdom of darkness, the castles and the dungeons of cyber space. I ask you to sever all ties, unhook the hooks, and wipe out the footprints in the spirit as well as all passwords that I used.

I ask You to remove all information in the files, records, back-ups, disks, etc. at the various websites and in Satan's satellite system in the heavenlies as well as all evidence of my involvement and presence in the Cyber Space. (The computer where these sites were accessed has been defiled and the secret police registers everyone whom goes into porn sites. There are files now opened against the owner of the computer. SATAN'S RECORDS IN HIS OWN SATELITE STATION IN THE HEAVENLIES!!)

Father, I petition that You remove my passport from every gatekeeper assigned at every gate way to the websites and also from Satan's satelite station. Father, I petition that sacrifices given to worship at this altar will be redeemed: time, relationships, commitment to You, etc.

Father, I repent of all the worship given not only to Asmodee (Jezebel & Lillith) but also the worship given to Mammon. (This money goes to the storerooms of Satan. The Power demon, Mammon, controls the storerooms of Satan from where he distributes all the gifts brought to Satan through sacrifices. In return he rewards the giver with mainly three gifts: sex, power and money).

Father, I petition that all the money sowed in to this kingdom through this form of worship will be cleansed and redeemed for Your Kingdom. (Entering into world of rapists, women abusers, children rapists, porn Mafia kingdom, porn and drug lords, money was given to these networks to trade with souls, women and children who are held as sex slaves to satisfy the lusts and perversions of men (Rev 18:13).

I ask Your forgiveness for this, in Jesus Name. Father, any code or secret name I was given, I renounce and ask you to remove it from me in Jesus Name. I petition in the Name of Jesus that You will remove and deliver me from all sexual powers, gifts, sex magic and magical charm. These demonic were used against me through this sin to seduce me as a victim. I pray that You will cleanse me and I rededicate my sexuality back unto You in Jesus Name.

I ask that You will purify my body, soul and spirit with the Blood of Jesus. Lord I want to present my body as a living sacrifice, holy and acceptable to You. I call upon Your Name Yahweh ELiashib – Lord, I pray that You will restore my soul in the Name of Jesus.

I petition, Father, that You will help me to hate this sin as You hate it. I know Your Word says that the beginning of Wisdom is to fear the Lord and the fear of the Lord is to hate sin. Prov 8:13 & 9:10.

Father, I petition You to severe all ungodly soul-ties between myself and any spiritual husbands or wives, personalities in pictures, imprints, names, or other ways of being connected, in Jesus' Name.

I petition, Father, that You will declare any ungodly marriages null and void and destroy all rings, clothing, contracts, covenants, names, titles, jewelry, and gifts – physically as well as spiritually – with Your Holy Spirit fire, in Jesus' Name.

I repent for defiling my marriage (if unmarried – future spouse) and for being unfaithful to my spouse. Also for defiling and breaking of the holiness with which You have created the institution of the marriage. I ask You Father that You will cleanse, purify, and restore my marriage and our marriage-bed altar in Jesus' Name.

I petition, Father that You will remove all seed still standing as evidence against me and my marriage, in Jesus' Name, and that You will remove any spiritual children from Satan's hands and take them to where you choose, in Jesus' Name.

Father, I petition that decoders will be placed at all entrances of my body, soul and spirit inclined to respond to certain codes or triggers. I ask you to de-activate the triggers like, tone of voices, sound waves, adverts, movies, songs, pictures, eyes, place, names, words, perfume, emotions, or touch, in Jesus Name.

• • • •

FATHER, I PETITION that You will enter my imagination area and sweep it clean with

Your Broom of Destruction. That You will place Your angels as gatekeepers and fire

all other gatekeepers.

Father, I repent for making a covenant with Asmodee (Jezebel and Lilith) through this sin. I ask that You will severe the five cords of Jezebel that controlled me for so long in the Name of Jesus. I also ask that You will shut and seal the gateways to Lilith and that You will purify my dream world. I ask that You will break the power of Asmodee over my life and that You will dismantle and destroy all ties with this Power demon.

Father, I repent for allowing idolatry in my life – self-love, lust, perversion, fornication, adultery and fantasy. Also for allowing the following spirits to rule me: a lying spirit, a perverse spirit and a spirit of whoredoms.

I also repent for worshipping the god named Eros and for taking part in tantric sex. Because of this sin I have opened myself to be possessed by the Kundalini spirit. I pray that You will close every chakra that was opened in the Name of Jesus. Please forgive me and deliver me from this evil spirit in Jesus Name.

I call upon Your Name Yahweh ELiphelet – Lord You are my Deliverance. Father I pray according to Isaiah 10:27 that the burden will be taken away from my shoulder, and that You will destroy the yoke from my neck with the anointing oil of Your Spirit. I ask this in the Name of Jesus Christ.

Father, I ask that You will strengthen my will and cause it to come into agreement with Your will. I choose to submit to You and to resist the evil one. I thank You Lord that You promise that those who humble themselves under the Mighty Hand of God will be exalted in due time (1 Pet 5:6). I declare that You are Yahweh ELuzai – You are my Strength!

I ask You to silence all witnesses testifying against me in the spirit by blotting out this sin with the precious Blood of Jesus. According to Job 31:1, I dictate a covenant (an agreement) to my eyes that I will not look [lustfully] upon a girl in the Name of Jesus.

Father, I petition that You will protect me from the consequences of the demonic prophecies, covenants, etc. Father, I petition that You will protect me from any punishment or judgment that will come into effect as a result of this petition. I petition all this in the Mighty Name of Jesus! AMEN.

Commanding Prayer to silence evil dreams, marine altars, and sexual demons.

There is power in commanding, the word is in your mouth, the word of authority and power vested by Jesus Christ. As you have the spirit of prophecy in you, the spirit of truth, you can bring light to any darkness. Any part of your life that is in darkness must be translated to light.

As the Son of God translated us from darkness to light, through faith we change our situation from worse to better, at all times trusting in the Lord. the Lord God moves when faith is exercised.

Job 38:12-13 Hast thou commanded the morning since thy days; and caused the
dayspring to know his place;
13 That it might take hold of the ends of the earth, that the wicked might be
shaken out of it?

You can command your morning to bring you glory. You can command the night to bring you honor that the arrows of the night be far from you and your family. Some powers won't leave you if you come with sweet prayers. When you are in spiritual warfare you are in a real fight like physical warfare. But in warfare, we are girded with mighty weapons to defeat the enemy.

Your prayer must shake the wicked out of your garden. Your prayer must shake the evil out of your land. The wicked spirits must leave your life and the life of your family members. The will of God is the redemption of souls out of Egypt.

Those who hunger and thirst righteousness shall be filled. Through the tongue, there is life and death. Your word has the power to move mountains, to shake the unshakable, and to give life to the impossible.

• • • •

HERE ARE 110 PRAYERS to shift your life.

1. I shut the doors that the marine agents and marine spirits use to infiltrate my spirit, soul, and body through dreams in the name of Jesus Christ.
2. I break the way through the waters in the name of Jesus Christ.
3. I have authority over the land, the sea, and over the fowl of the air in the mighty name of Jesus.
4. These land, the sea, and the air are for the Lord, anything that is against me is brought to shame in the name of the LORD.
5. My left foot is on the land, my right foot is on the sea and my right hand is towards the heavens, I decree and declare in the name of the Lord that no weapon formed against me from the land, water, and air shall prosper in the name of Jesus Christ.
6. Every evil alter that cooks dreams and presents them to me at night, is destroyed in the name of Jesus.
7. I issue divorce papers to any queen of the water to sleep with me in dreams in the name of Jesus.
8. Any spiritual marriage that happens in any way without my knowledge, be broken in the mighty name of Jesus Christ.

9. Any object of the covenant in my body in the realm of spirit, be removed in the mighty name of Jesus Christ of Nazareth.

10. My spirit, soul, and body are sanctified by the precious blood of Jesus Christ.

11. The Lord God is my great light, light up my world, and lit up my candle.

12. My spirit is intertwined with the Holy Spirit in the name of Jesus.

13. Fire within me will destroy any power that touches me in the night in the name of Jesus Christ.

14. I am the bride of Jesus Christ; I divorce any idol right now in the great name of the Holy Father.

15. Every evil arrow that comes from the East, West, North, and South, falls down in the name of Jesus Christ.

16. The sun and the moon shall not smite me in the name of Jesus Christ.

17. Every spirit wife/ every spirit husband, dies, in the name of Jesus.

18. Everything you have deposited in my life, come out by fire, in the name of Jesus.

19. Every power that is working against my marriage, falls down and dies, in the name of Jesus.

20. I divorce and renounce my marriage with the spirit husband or wife, in the name of Jesus.

21. I break all covenants entered into with the spirit husband or wife, in the name of Jesus.

22. I command the thunder fire of God to burn to ashes the wedding gown, ring, photographs and all other materials used for the marriage, in Jesus' name.

23. I send the fire of God to burn to ashes the marriage certificate, in the name of Jesus.

24. I break every blood and soul-tie covenants with the spirit husband or wife, in the name of Jesus.

25. I send thunder fire of God to burn to ashes the children born to the marriage, in Jesus' name.

26. I withdraw my blood, sperm or any other part of my body deposited on the altar of the spirit husband or wife, in Jesus name.

27. You spirit husband or wife tormenting my life and earthly marriage I bind you with hot chains and fetters of God and cast you out of my life into the deep pit, and I command you not to ever come into my life again, in the name of Jesus.

28. I return to you, every property of yours in my possession in the spirit world, including the dowry and whatsoever was used for the marriage and covenants, in the name of Jesus.

29. I drain myself of all evil materials deposited in my body as a result of our sexual relation, in Jesus' name.

30. Lord, send Holy Ghost fire into my root and burn out all unclean things deposited in it by the spirit husband or wife, in the name of Jesus.

31. I break the head of the snake, deposited into my body by the spirit husband or wife to do me harm, and command it to come out, in the name of Jesus.

32. I purge out, with the blood of Jesus, every evil material deposited in my womb to prevent me from having children on earth.

33. Lord, repair and restore every damage done to any part

of my body and my earthly marriage by the spirit husband or wife, in the name of Jesus.

34. I reject and cancel every curse, evil pronouncement, spell, jinx, enchantment and incantation place upon me by the spirit husband or wife, in the name of Jesus.

35. I take back and possess all my earthly belonging in the custody of the spirit husband or wife, in Jesus' name.

36. I command the spirit husband or wife to turn his or her back on me forever, in Jesus' name.

37. I renounce and reject the name given to me by the spirit husband or wife, in the name of Jesus.

38. I hereby declare and confess that the Lord Jesus Christ is my Husband for eternity, in Jesus' name.

39. I soak myself in the blood of Jesus and cancel the evil mark or writings placed on me, in Jesus' name.

40. I set myself free from the stronghold, domineering power and bondage of the spirit husband or wife, in the name of Jesus.

41. I paralyze the remote control power and work used to destabilize my earthly marriage and to hind me from bearing children for my earthly husband or wife, in the name of Jesus.

42. I announce to the heavens that I am forever married to Jesus.

43. Every trademark of evil marriage, be shaken out of my life, in the name of Jesus.

44. Every evil writing, engraved by iron pen, be wiped off by the blood of Jesus.

45. I bring the blood of Jesus upon the spirit that does not want to go, in the name of Jesus.

46. I bring the blood of Jesus on every evidence that can be tendered by wicked spirits against me.

47. I file a counter-report in the heavens against every evil marriage, in the name of Jesus.

48. I refuse to supply any evidence that the enemy may use against me, in the name of Jesus.

49. 33. Let satanic exhibitions be destroyed by the blood of Jesus.

50. I declare to you spirit wife/ husband that there is no vacancy for you in my life, in the name of Jesus.

51. O Lord, make me a vehicle of deliverance.

52. I come by faith to mount Zion Lord, command deliverance upon my life now.

53. Lord, water me from the waters of God. 38. Let the careful siege of the enemy be dismantled, in Jesus name

54. O Lord, defend your interest in my life.

55. Everything, written against me in the cycle of the moon, be blotted out, in Jesus' name.

56. Everything, programmed into the sun, moon and stars against me, be dismantled, in Jesus' name.

57. Every evil thing programmed into my genes, be blotted out by the blood of Jesus.

58. O Lord, shake out seasons of failure and frustrations from my life.

59. I overthrow every wicked law, working against my life, in the name of Jesus.

60. I ordain a new time, season and profitable law, in Jesus' name.

61. I speak destruction unto the palaces of the queen of the coast and of the rivers, in Jesus' name.

62. I speak destruction unto the headquarters of the spirit of Egypt and blow up their altars, in the name of Jesus.

63. I speak destruction unto the altars, speaking against the purpose of God for my life, in Jesus' name.

64. I declare myself a virgin for the Lord, in Jesus' name.

65. Let every evil veil upon my life be torn open, in Jesus' name.

66. Every wall between me and the visitation of God, be broken, in the name of Jesus.

67. Let the counsel of God proper in my life, in the name of Jesus.

68. I destroy the power of any demonic seed in my life from the womb, in the name of Jesus.

69. I speak unto my umbilical gate to over throw all negative parental spirits, in the name of Jesus.

70. I break the yoke of the spirit, having access to my reproductive gates, in the name of Jesus.

71. O Lord, let your time of refreshing come upon me.

72. I bring fire from the altar of the Lord upon every evil marriage, in the name of Jesus.

73. I redeem myself by the blood of Jesus from every sex trap, in the name of Jesus.

74. I erase the engraving of my name on any evil marriage record, in the name of Jesus'.

75. I reject and renounce every evil spiritual marriage, in the name of Jesus.

76. I confess that Jesus is my original spouse and is jealous over me.

77. I issue a bill of divorcement to every spirit wife/husband, in the name of Jesus.

78. I bind ever spirit wife/ husband with everlasting chains, in the name of Jesus.

79. Let heavenly testimony overcome every evil testimony of hell, in the name of Jesus.

80. O Lord, bring to my remembrance every spiritual trap and contract.

81. Let the blood of Jesus purge me of every contaminating material, in the name of Jesus.

82. Let the spirit husband/wife fall down and die, in Jesus name.

83. Let all your children attached to me fall down and die, in the name of Jesus.

84. I burn your certificates and destroy your rings, in Jesus name.

85. I execute judgment against water spirits and declare that you are reserved for everlasting chains in darkness, in Jesus name.

86. O Lord, contend with those who are contending with me.

87. Every trademark of water spirit, be shaken out of my life, in the name of Jesus.

88. Every clone in the water that is representing me, be destroyed by fire in the name of Jesus.

89. Every semen of mine stored in the kingdom of darkness, by the blood of Christ be vanished.

90. Every name of mine written in the kingdom of darkness be erased by the power of the blood of Jesus Christ.

91. I speak the spirit of resurrection upon the water over my blessings swallowed by the marine agents, locate me in the name of Jesus.

92. Bars of the underworld carrying every aspect of my soul, be broken in the mighty name of the Lord.

93. Let the soul snatcher be confounded in the mighty name of Jesus Christ.

94. Spirit of death and hades leave me in the mighty name of Jesus Christ.

95. Spirit of ignorance and darkness leave me in the mighty name of Jesus Christ.

96. Let the occult priesthood be brought to shame in my life the mighty name of Jesus Christ.

97. Marine spiritual doctors be devoured by the mighty sword in the name of Jesus Christ.

98. Every programme in the water against my destiny, be exposed in the mighty name of Jesus Christ.

99. Blood of Jesus Christ speaks better things over my soul and over my family.

100. Every good thing shall manifest in my life in the mighty name of Jesus Christ.

101. Grace and mercy of the Lord locate me.

102. Favor and prosperity of the Lord locate me by fire.

103. The goodness of the Lord locates me.

104. Free me from harm.

105. In blessing me, bless me.

106. The shepherd of my spirit, soul and body, covers me with your great light of wisdom, knowledge and understanding.

107. Strengthen my inner man.

108. Quicken my spirit man.

109. I decree and I declare that whatsoever that is written in the books of destinies concerning my life, shall come to

pass.

110. It is well with my soul in the mighty name of Jesus
Christ.

Destructive fire prayers against Marine marriage breakers.

Father, in the Name of Jesus Christ of Nazareth, Your living Son, I come before Your throne to petition for my marriage. Thank You that, according to Your Word in Ps 20:4 and I John 5:5, You will grant me my petitions.

Father, in the Name of Jesus Christ I confirm my covenant with You. I also confirm the covenant between my marriage partner and me. I confess that my marriage covenant was sealed by the Blood of the Lamb and that He alone is worthy to ever break the seals.

I come before Your throne to petition against any curses of divorce or adultery. I pray that You would break these curses and change them into blessings. I cut my marriage loose from the spirit of death that wants to bring death and destruction to my marriage.

I petition against the spirit of Jezebel. I forbid her to have any authority over my marriage. In the Name of Jesus, I petition before Your throne that the Blood of Jesus would wipe our names from the book of the whore of Babylon. I confess that our names are written in the Book of Life in the New Jerusalem.

In the presence of Your throne I declare a divorce from the Cup of Jezebel. If we or any of our forefathers have drunk from her cup, I ask You now to cleanse us - spirit, soul and body - from any poison coming from this cup. I ask that the Fire of the Holy Spirit would come to destroy the influence of this cup over our lives.

I PETITION AGAINST any marriage contracts with any human spirits, dead human spirits, demons and any spiritual husbands or wives. I sever the soul ties and declare a divorce in the spirit. I ask the Fire of the Holy Spirit to destroy any physical or spiritual rings. I declare Hosea 2: 5-6 over any third person who might be sent against my marriage.

I petition against the Ancient Serpent, bewitchment, spirits of deception and seduction. I cancel any orders given to them with regard to my marriage and declare them null and void in the Name of Jesus Christ of Nazareth.

I petition against any rituals against my marriage. In the Name of Jesus I break the power of the rituals and the seals placed upon them. Thank You, Father, that You now reverse all those rituals in the spirit. I petition against any form of sexual magic.

I petition against any defilement of seed. I pray that all seed testifying against us in the physical or in the spiritual, would be destroyed by the Fire of the Holy Spirit. I petition against the god of this world, the spirit of this world and the mind of this world. I cancel any authority given to this spirit over my marriage and declare that the purposes, will and plan of the Almighty God, the Father of Abraham, Isaac and Jacob, will be fulfilled in my marriage.

I petition against any plans of Abaddon and Baal over my marriage. I break any traps or snares set against us in the physical or in the spiritual and render them powerless in the Name of Jesus Christ of Nazareth.

I petition against any programming against my marriage in the sun, moon, stars and planets. I ask You to destroy those programs with the Blood of Jesus Christ of Nazareth.

Father, in the Name of Jesus Christ of Nazareth I now petition before Your throne that any of Satan's petitions against my marriage would now be thrown out of the heavenly courtroom. I ask this on account of the price that Jesus paid on the cross.

I petition against any hex, spell, curse, chanting, incantation and white, black, red and green magic being used against my marriage.

I petition that Your voice would now thunder in the heavenlies with regard to my marriage; that Your light and truth would prevail over my marriage. I pray that Your voice would now declare in the heavenlies that none of Satan's petitions against my marriage would be granted.

Father, in the Name of Jesus Christ of Nazareth I now declare my marriage to be sealed by the Blood of Jesus. Thank You that You have spoken Your blessing over my marriage. Father, in the Name of Jesus I pray that there would be love, unity and peace in my marriage.

Thank you, Father, that Your Holy Spirit watches over my marriage.

AMEN.

ALPHA AND OMEGA – Israel Houghton
[verse: 1]
You are Alpha and Omega
We worship you our Lord
you are worthy to be praised
[chorus]
We give you all the glory
we worship you our Lord
you are worthy to be praised

. . . .

WHAT THE LORD HAS DONE IN ME – HILLSONG
[VERSE: 1]
Let the weak say, "I am strong"
Let the poor say, "I am rich"
Let the blind say, "I can see"
It's what the Lord has done in me
[CHORUS]
Hosanna, hosanna
To the Lamb that was slain
Hosanna, hosanna
Jesus died and rose again
[VERSE: 2]
To the river I will wade
There my sins are washed away
From the heavens' mercy streams
Of the Savior's love for me

[VERSE: 3]
I will rise from waters deep
Into the saving arms of God
I will sing salvation songs
Jesus Christ has set me free
[CHORUS]
Hosanna, hosanna
To the Lamb that was slain
Hosanna, hosanna
Jesus died and rose again

· · · ·

BE LIFTED UP – PAUL AOKLEY
[CHORUS]
Be lifted up, be lifted up
As we bow down,
Be lifted up.
(Repeat)
[VERSE:1]
Let the heavens rejoice
Let the nations be glad
Let the whole earth tremble
For you are God
Come and worship the Lord
In the beauty of holiness
As we bow down,
Be lifted up,
As we bow down,
Be lifted up

• • • •

I WILL EXALT YOU – BROOKE FRASER
[Verse: 1]
I will exalt You
I will exalt You
I will exalt You
You are my God
[Chorus]
My hiding place My safe refuge
My treasure Lord You are
My friend and King Anointed One
Most Holy.
[Verse: 2]
Because You're with me
Because You're with me
Because You're with me
I will not fear

• • • •

AWESOME GOD – SINACH
Holy are you Lord
All creation call you God
Worthy is your name
We worship Your Majesty
Awesome God, how great thou art
You are God, mighty are Your miracles
We stand in awe of your holy name
Lord we bow and worship You
King of kings, Lord of lords, everlasting Kind

Savior Redeemer, Soon coming King
King of kings, Lord of lords, everlasting Kind
Savior Redeemer, Soon coming King
Awesome, awesome, You are awesome
Awesome, awesome, You are awesome
...
Awesome is your name.

. . . .

BECAUSE YOU LIVE – SINACH
[VERSE: 1]
You paid the price
The highest price
Am so grateful
For your love
You took my place
Now I stand
To be called your very own
[CHORUS]
Because you live
Jesus I live
I have no fear
Of what tomorrow brings
Because you live
Jesus I live today
I live to praise your name
I live to praise your name
I have no fear of what tomorrow brings

. . . .

WELCOME IN THIS PLACE – HILLSONG
Holy Spirit, Holy Spirit
Comforter Counsellor here
Holy Spirit sent from heaven
The God of all glory is here
Rise up within me
Living Water, Spirit of God in me
You are welcome in this place
You are welcome in this place
God of power love and grace
Saturate my soul
You are welcome in this place
You are welcome in this place
Holy Spirit guide my way
Saturate my soul
Closest Friend
Here in Your presence
Is fullness of joy overflowing

• • • •

YOU ARE MY STRENGTH – HILLSONG
You are my strength
Strength like no other
Strength like no other
Reaches to me
You are my hope
Hope like no other
Hope like no other
Reaches to me
In the fullness of Your grace

In the power of Your Name
You lift me up
You lift me up
Unfailing love
Stronger than mountains
Deeper than oceans
Reaches to me
Your love O Lord
Reaches to the heavens
Your faithfulness
Reaches to the skies

• • • •

WORTHY IS THE LAMB – HILLSONG
VERSE: 1
Thank you for the cross Lord
Thank you for the price You paid
Bearing all my sin and shame
In love You came
And gave amazing grace
VERSE: 2
Thank you for this love Lord
Thank you for the nail pierced hands
Washed me in Your cleansing flow
Now all I know
Your forgiveness and embrace
CHORUS:
Worthy is the Lamb
Seated on the throne
Crown You now with many crown

You reign victorious
High and lifted up
Jesus Son of God
The Darling of Heaven crucified
Worthy is the Lamb
Worthy is the Lamb

• • • •

DAYS OF ELIJAH – ROBIN MARK
These are the days of Elijah
Declaring the Word of the Lord
And these are the days of your servant Moses
Righteousness being restored
And though these are days of great trials
Of famine and darkness and sword
Still we are the voice in the desert crying
Prepare ye the way of the Lord!
Behold He comes! Riding on the clouds!
Shining like the sun! At the trumpet call
Lift your voice! It's the year of Jubilee!
And out of Zion's hill salvation comes!
And these are the days of Ezekiel
The dry bones becoming as flesh
And these are the days of your servant David
Rebuilding a temple of praise
And these are the days of the harvest
The fields are as white in the world
And we are the labourers in your vineyard
Declaring the word of the Lord!
Behold He comes! Riding on the clouds!

Shining like the sun! At the trumpet call
Lift your voice! It's the year of Jubilee!
And out of Zion's hill salvation comes!
There's no God like Jehovah!
There's no God like Jehovah!
There's no God like Jehovah!
There's no God like Jehovah!
(Repeat 3 times)
Behold He comes! Riding on the clouds!
Shining like the sun! At the trumpet call
Lift your voice! It's the year of Jubilee!
And out of Zion's hill salvation comes!

HOSANNA HOSANNA

Hosanna, Hosanna, Hosanna in the highest
Hosanna, Hosanna, Hosanna in the highest
Lord we lift up Your Name,
With hearts full of praise,
Be exalted Oh Lord our God,
Hosanna in the highest.
Glory, Glory, Glory to the King of Kings
Glory, Glory, Glory to the King of Kings
Lord we lift up Your Name,
With hearts full of praise,
Be exalted Oh Lord our God,
Glory to the King of Kings.

• • • •

MY REDEEMER LIVES – HILLSONG

I know he rescued my soul
His blood has covered my sins

I believe, I believe
My shame he's taken away
My pain is healed in his name
I believe, I belive
Coda:
I'll raise a banner, (oh.. hoh) cause my lord
Has conquered the grave
Chorus:
My redeemer lives, my redeemer lives
My redeemer lives, my redeemer lives
(Repeat 1st and 2nd verse)
(Repeat coda and chorus)
Bridge:
You lift my burden, I'll rise with you
I'm dancing on this mountain top
To see your kingdom come
(Repeat chorus)

• • • •

ANCIENT OF DAYS – RON KENOLY
Blessing and Honour
Glory and Power
Be unto the ancient of days
From every nation
All of creation
Bow before the ancient of days
Bridge:
Every tongue in heaven and earth
Shall declare your glory
Every knee shall bow at your throne

In worship
You will be exalted oh God
And your kingdom shall not pass away
Oh ancient of days
Chorus:
Your kingdom shall reign over all the earth
Sing to the ancient of days
For none can compare to your matchless worth
Sing to the ancient of days
(Bridge and Chorus again)

. . . .

CELEBRATE JESUS CELEBRATE – DON MOEN

Celebrate Jesus celebrate
Celebrate Jesus celebrate
Celebrate Jesus celebrate
Celebrate Jesus celebrate
He is risen
He is risen
And He lives forevermore
He is risen
He is risen
Come on and celebrate
Come on and celebrate
Come on and celebrate
The resurrection of our Lord

Altar of incense for your victory.

Altar of incense is your rising worship towards the heavenly, where the seat of authority for all mankind is.

Romans 12:1 I beseech you therefore, brethren, by the mercies of God, that ye present
your bodies a living sacrifice, holy, acceptable unto God, which is your
reasonable service.

Now it is pretty clear that our bodies are the living sacrifice. When we worship, praise, and offer thanksgiving to the Lord God, we are presenting ourselves before His throne as a living sacrifice.

We are already set apart by the precious blood of Jesus Christ. We have moved from being self-righteous to totally dependent on the righteousness of God, which is the greatest gift to mankind.

I assure you that if you claim the blood of Christ as your covering and as your shield against the wiles of the enemy, you shall put to shame the wicked spirits that harass you from time to time.

Our prayers ascend to heaven like smoke. Especially when we praise and worship, the heavenly atmosphere changes. Worships attract angels. Many times when believers worship, the heavens are opened.

The glory of God comes down on us like a mighty rain. In the midst of despair and difficulties, raise your flag of victory up high. The Lord God of Israel inhabits the praises of His people. You are His people. One man or woman is a great army to the Lord.

Never allow fear to overrule your faith, always keep the faith. In the ancient days many wars were won by the Israelites and Judah by proclaiming "His mercy endures forever". Wars are fought and won through prayers. Ascend and transcend in prayer. Keep burning in the love for God!

And when he had taken the book, the four beasts and four and twenty
elders fell down before the Lamb, having every one of them harps, and golden
vials full of odours, which are the prayers of saints.
Revelation 5:8.

Even in heaven angels and the redeemed praise and worship the living King. Prayers smell as a sweet aroma before the presence of God. Prayers that align with the will of God will always be answered. Go into the throne room for mercy and grace. The blood of Christ is our advocate. The blood speaks better things than the blood of Abel. Grace, mercy, favor, peace, and prosperity shall follow you.

Philippians 1:11 Being filled with the fruits of righteousness,
which are by Jesus Christ,
unto the glory and praise of God.

Revelation 5:9 reveals that we are kings and priests. The responsibility of a king is to rule and reign in power and glory like King David was, while the responsibility of a priest is to offer sacrifices and incense unto the Lord.

Offer your bodies as the living sacrifice to the Lord.
Revelation 5:9 And they sung a new song, saying, Thou art worthy to take the book, and
to open the seals thereof: for thou wast slain, and hast redeemed us to God by
thy blood out of every kindred, and tongue, and people, and na-tion; 10 And hast
made us unto our God kings and priests: and we shall reign on the earth.

• • • •

NOTES.

Prayers From Spirit Wives and Spirit Husbands by Dr D. K. Olukoya.

Don't miss out!

Visit the website below and you can sign up to receive emails whenever Johannes Tefo publishes a new book. There's no charge and no obligation.

https://books2read.com/r/B-A-UEZX-FLKJD

BOOKS 2 READ

Connecting independent readers to independent writers.

Did you love *Deliverance From Sexual Dreams*? Then you should read *Battle In The Sea: How To Tackle Spiritual Warfare And Win The Battle*[1] by Johannes Tefo!

[2]

This is a must-have book about how to tackle spiritual warfare and win in the name of the LORD. Through this profound book, you will come out armed with strategic prayers to silence the powers that have been harassing' and messing with your life. The marine kingdom is one of the deadliest kingdoms of Satan, located under the sea. This book came through a revelation. As someone who has been the victim of evil, as we all are, the LORD has been gracious to me, teaching my hands how to wage

---

1. https://books2read.com/u/49aE5X

2. https://books2read.com/u/49aE5X

the right warfare against the enemy. Through years of experience and the work of the Holy Spirit, this is the book to amplify your inner man and strengthen you in times like this. Believers have to take territory, win souls, and deliver captives, this is a must-have book filled with wisdom and knowledge for your spiritual deliverance.

Also by Johannes Tefo

Family spiritual Warfare Books
Generational Curses And Spiritual Warfare: Spiritual Strategies
& Principles Of Victory Against Evil Strongholds
Youth's Guide To Spiritual Warfare
A Women's Guide To Spiritual Warfare

Standalone
Deliver Your Soul From Evil
Overcoming Spirit Of Stagnation
The 24: Prophetic Word For This Season 2024 And Beyond
Michael For Warfare
Territorial Spirits: Overcome Evil Strongholds in Your Life And
Take Over Your Community With Strategic Warfare And Win-
ning Prayers
Prayers Against Suicide Spirit
Spiritual Warfare When Enough is Enough
Identity In Christ
Prayers Against Satanic Networks

The Workplace You Need: Spiritual Warfare Prayers That Silence Evil Powers At Your Workplace.

Deliverance From Mind Control: Be Free And Delivered From Every Marine Demons Of Mind Control

Times Getting Hard: Scriptures Of Comfort For Hard Days

Battle In The Sea: How To Tackle Spiritual Warfare And Win The Battle

Freedom: Deliverance Of Souls From Captivity

A Dedicated Prayer Lifestyle: Simple Tips To Effective Prayer Lifestyle

Deliverance From Sexual Dreams

Sexual Lust, Demons, And Impurity

Redefined By Fire: Unleashing The Power Of The Holy Spirit Within.

About the Author

Before he started writing Christian books, Johannes got a graduate degree in Film and Television from university of Johannesburg. After that, just to shake things up, he went to equip himself with religious studies, particularly Christianity, just to have knack about the world beyond the curtains of time. And how this body of Christ has transformed millions of people around the world, not neglecting how sadly the movement has been persecuted from time to time. He now writes full time.